THANK YOU

SKATEBOARDING

THANK YOU

SKATEBOARDING

RICKY ROBERTS III

IP INDEPENDENTLY PUBLISHED

Cover Design: Keith Burnson
Editor: Jeanie Lyubelsky
Bio & Cover Photo: Chris Stone

Published in the United States of America
1. Individual Sports / Skateboarding
2. Sports & Recreation / Skateboarding
20.02.20

CONTENTS

DEDICATION

This book is dedicated to all skateboarders—those who currently skate or once did—and to those who encourage and support skateboarders.

Thank you all for being a part of making skateboarding, in all ways, amazing.

PREFACE

Skateboarding has done so much for my life, as I bet it has also done for yours—current and former skateboarders. I feel inspired to write this book as a testament of my appreciation and thanks for skateboarding and the many ways it has contributed to my overall well-being. This is my way of saying: "Thank you skateboarding!"

INTRODUCTION

Around eleven years old, I rode a skateboard for the first time. At the time, I raced BMX bikes pretty seriously and was ranked number two in the state and eighth in the nation for my division. Bike racing was the only activity I had an interest in, until I rode a skateboard on that special day. I was drawn to skateboarding instantly. Even though I didn't have a skateboard of my own, I knew I wanted to skate again.

Before long, I ended up with someone's old board. I brought it to every BMX race I went to from then on. The only thing I would think about when I was at the races was riding my skateboard.

I enjoyed BMX racing and the people I met doing it, but skateboarding spoke to me in a way that I couldn't ignore. As my thoughts of skateboarding overshadowed racing, my bike time started to feel more like a burden than something I wanted to do. Not long after being introduced to skateboarding, I stopped wanting to go away racing on weekends, because it meant I couldn't skate as much as I wanted to.

Finally the week came when I decided not to race; instead, I went skateboarding all weekend. That was it! From that point on, I knew I wanted to spend as much time as possible on my skateboard. I eventually quit racing to put all of my attention on skateboarding.

I got my first new 'complete' for my twelfth birthday. It was a Powell Peralta, Tony Hawk, with T-Bone wheels and Independent Trucks (this was 1988, to give you a better visual of the board). Getting a new board motivated me; I started to push myself harder than ever to progress, as skateboarding became all I thought about. I watched as many skate videos as I could and looked through every skate magazine that I could get my hands on. I skated any chance I had. If I wasn't in school, I was skateboarding. I skated before school and right after. No matter how sore or tired I got, I still skated and would get super bummed if I wasn't able to do so. I could never get enough of skateboarding back then and still feel like I can't now.

As a youth, skateboarding was my biggest passion and the thing I was most focused on, and it was also my refuge. There are many layers to the details of my childhood, some of which I will share later in the book. To keep it short for now, I experienced abuse on many levels, witnessed much violence, and lived in poverty. I was angry and felt alone.

No matter how hard things were at different times in my life, when I got on my skateboard, I always felt better. Through some of my lowest points, I wanted to close myself off from the world, but my passion for skateboarding motivated me to get out of the house and go skate. Once on my skateboard, I would go from being unhappy to feeling excited. To this day, skateboarding still keeps me inspired.

At this point in my life, I have gone through many different phases of skateboarding. As years passed by, there were many times I would skate heavily for a few weeks or months and then stop again. The cycle of starting and stopping went on for many years. Even though I skated sporadically through the years, there was never a time since I got my first board that I didn't have one and at least skate a bit, even if it was only once every few months. No matter how far I drifted from skating, I always found myself going back to it. In fact, I have never stopped being drawn to skateboarding since the first time I tried it over thirty years ago.

In recent years, a new skatepark opened near my house (St. Pete Skatepark). I fell in love with it right away and felt inspired to put more time into skating again. Since the park opened, I have been skating on a regular basis, which feels great. I definitely lost many tricks from not skating frequently over the years, but that is to be expected. Although it gets frustrating to not be able to do something you have done multiple times in the past, I enjoy the process of relearning tricks I could once do and learning some new ones. It's been a humbling yet awesome journey, for sure. Beyond working on getting old tricks back and learning new ones, I started to appreciate and take special notice of the many different benefits of skateboarding, which I will share with you in the following pages.

Whether you currently skate or once did, I think you will appreciate my perspectives and be able to relate on many levels. If you are not a skateboarder but have one in your life, this book will give you a deeper insight into skateboarding—what some of its benefits are and why those of us who skate are so driven to do so. Whatever your situation may be, I hope my thoughts about skateboarding and the many positive impacts it has on my life, as well as the lives of so many others, reaches you well and gives you an even greater appreciation for skateboarding than you already have.

Before I go on, and since I shared some of my history and connection to skateboarding, I think it is important for you to reflect on yours a bit too. Please take some time to consider the following questions.

How long have you been skateboarding, or how long did you skate before you stopped?

How were you first introduced to skateboarding?

What was your first board like, and how old were you when you got it?

What was the first trick you learned?

What did it, or does it, feel like for you to be on a skateboard?

What are some of your favorite memories of skateboarding?

How many of the friends that you have now did you meet through skateboarding?

How has skateboarding influenced your life?

DETERMINATION

Looking at skateboarding from outside of it makes it easy to question if skating is worth it and why people would risk getting hurt to do it. Think about what most skateboarders look like after a long skate session. Chances are that they will be all sweaty, have dirty clothes, and at least one bruise or scratch somewhere on their body—not to mention that their shoes usually look like they need to be thrown away. A person that doesn't skateboard, or at least doesn't know what it takes to do it, may be quick to judge them. What most people don't

understand is that the scratches, b
dirty clothes on a skateboarder's b
with holes in their shoes, represent un   ...ng
amounts of determination.

Skateboarders are some of the most driven
and determined people I know. Once their
minds are made up on something, they become
so determined that they will usually not stop
until it happens, no matter what. Think about
how long it took you to learn certain tricks
you've done. How many times have you been
hurting, but you kept going until you landed
the trick you were trying?

I have had many experiences in skating
when I felt like giving up on a trick before I
did it. A recent example comes to mind. I was
trying a frontside lip slide across the top of a
manual pad. The ledge is about one and half
feet tall, and the manual pad is about ten to
twelve feet long. Because of the direction I
was sliding from, I had to pop over a step at
the end to come off of the ledge. I struggled
to get it. After about forty-five minutes into
the battle, I was covered in sweat, sore, and

exhausted. I felt like quitting.

In order for me to keep pushing to land the trick, my determination had to overpower the feelings and thoughts I had about giving up. I felt discouraged—like I wanted to stop trying—but I kept pushing on anyway. I was determined to land the trick and couldn't let anything stop me, even though my thoughts to do so were appealing in the moment. Lip sliding the ledge over the manual pad took me well over an hour to do, but I eventually landed it!

Although I harnessed the determination to do the trick, I didn't push through the desire to quit alone. I had the support and motivation from friends that were also there skating, which helped immensely. I will get more into the power of the support skateboarders give each other later in the book.

The determination I utilized to land that trick is not unique to me. How I see it, is that anyone who decides to put in the time and effort to learn anything beyond being able to stand on a skateboard or simply riding it down the street has a lot of determination to start with, and their motivation gets stronger the more they skate. The amount of determination that skateboarders have continues to inspire me to this day. The fact that we can apply that same level of determination in all parts of our life makes me appreciate skateboarding even more.

Skateboarding challenges you to your core, as does life. The same determination you have (or had when you skated) to learn new tricks on a skateboard can be used to achieve anything you put your mind to. Not only can the determination skateboarders have be harnessed to accomplish things outside of skating, it also helps give people mental toughness to get through whatever obstacles life brings. The determination I got from skateboarding has proven useful in virtually every area of my life, as I am sure has happened in yours.

Thank you skateboarding, for being a part of making us the determined people we are—capable of achieving anything we put our minds to.

PERSPECTIVE

If you skateboard for any significant amount of time, your perspective on life and what is possible changes. When you see a set of stairs, you don't see something to walk on, you see an obstacle to do a trick down. As a skateboarder, you see your surroundings much differently than people that never skated.

The perspective of possibilities you get (or got) from skateboarding also manifests in others areas of your life. For example, when obstacles come into your life, instead of being intimidated by them, you more than likely will find a way around them. Your default way of thinking can be formed through skateboarding; it helps you to look for possibilities of how to overcome hardships you face, rather than reasons to give up when those hardships arise.

Some of the most creative and innovative people I know either skateboard now or once did. From the moment someone gets their first skateboard, they begin to see the world differently, which ultimately cultivates the ability to see limitless possibilities of things to do, create, and achieve. I believe that after you skateboard for any significant amount of time, the perspectives you get on life, yourself, and the world around you through skateboarding are always a part of you—even if you no longer do it. Whether overcoming obstacles, creating art of any kind, exceling at work, starting a business, or living life in general, I believe that the different perspectives people get from skateboarding help them see creative and strategic ways to also do well in other areas of their lives.

People that skate, or once did, find solutions

to problems where there don't seem to be any. They create works of art and music that leave people in awe, excel in their chosen careers and establish businesses that are successful, start causes that are impactful, and so on. Skateboarders, generally speaking, stay true to themselves and to the life they want to live. I attribute, in part, the great things I have seen many skateboarders do in their lives to the enhanced perspective of possibilities that skateboarding gave them.

Thank you skateboarding, for giving us such a transformative perspective on life and what we are capable of achieving.

COMMUNITY

As I mentioned earlier, skateboarding became an escape for me, and the people I skated with were like family to me. We looked out for one another. I honestly can't count how many times I was out skating when I was younger and my friends shared their food and drinks with me because I didn't have money to buy my own at the time. There were also multiple occasions during my childhood when friends I skated with gave me their old skate decks, clothes, and shoes when I needed them.

I still see the same sense of support among

skateboarders today. It is not uncommon to see a stack of used shoes or boards left at the skatepark for someone in need to take. It is always gratifying for me to give another skateboarder my old deck when I set up a new one. Many skateboarders out there may not have the means to get new stuff. I know firsthand that any skateboarder in need is always appreciative for the support received from the skate community. I am forever grateful for the different people that gave me skating goods over the years, especially when I needed them most.

Beyond skateboarders being so generous with material belongings, the skateboard community is very welcoming. Generally speaking, the skate community accepts everyone. Have a good attitude, be respectful, and you're accepted. You can go anywhere in the world with your skateboard, and you will almost always be welcomed where there are other skateboarders skating. Occasionally, a skateboarder will make others feel like they are not welcome, but that is not the norm in the skate community.

When you look at the skateboard community as a collective, there is much to be learned from it. Skateboarding has one of the most diverse ranges of participants. Your age, weight, height, gender identity, socio-economic status, sexual orientation, religion, skin color, ethnicity, and skill level does not matter in the skateboarding community—everyone is welcomed and accepted for who they are. Skateboarders pretty much always respect, support, and encourage each other, despite their perceived differences. This is not to say that they all like one another, but it is rare for skateboarders to be mean or disrespectful to one another.

Thank you skateboarding, for bringing so many people together to create such a diverse and welcoming global community for us all to be a part of.

FOCUS

There is so much to calculate, assess, and incorporate into doing a trick on a skateboard. You have to calculate the appropriate speed, your body position, feet placement and how to kick them, when to pop, lift, spin, and more. Tricks in and out of obstacles, especially onto ledges or handrails, require an even greater level of precision than other tricks. Everything has to be just right, or the trick won't work, with the exception of the occasional 'ride away' that doesn't seem possible but happens anyway.

Beyond the adjustments you make with your body, board, and speed, you also have to assess the terrain and obstacles you're skating on. Are there any rocks or items on the ground that could make you fall? Is the obstacle waxed enough or maybe too slick for your preference? All of these observations and more are happening while you're calculating what needs to take place in order for you to do the trick you're trying.

The variables are different depending on where you are skating and how many other skateboarders, motorists, or pedestrians may be around at the time. Everything you have to assess and calculate in your mind is then incorporated into your physical motion while doing the trick. In some cases, this is all happening simultaneously with controlling your mind in order to overcome the fear of whatever trick you're doing. Whether you're conscious of it or not, your mind is always actively involved in helping you skate.

Your mind, like the muscles in your body, needs to be exercised on a regular basis in order to perform optimally. The more you exercise it, the stronger it becomes. Skateboarding is a phenomenal workout for your mind. Your mind exercises and enhances its ability to focus, which gives you an extraordinary capacity to learn, do, and create what interests you—especially with objectives that require much attention to detail. In other words, when you apply the intensity of focus that your mind requires to skateboard onto all areas of life, anything is possible.

Thank you skateboarding, for helping us develop such strong and focused minds that we can use to do amazing things in every aspect of our lives.

GETTING BACK UP

Falling is part of skateboarding. Chances are that you will fall at least once and probably more during every skate session you have. As a skateboarder, you understand that. You not only become okay with it, but in some ways, you come to expect it.

It is not uncommon to fall twenty or more times while learning a new trick. There are random instances when you learn a new trick on your first try, but not often; falling many times in the process is common. No matter how many times you fall, though, you keep getting back up, over and over again. You get back up as many times as it takes until you get the trick you are trying, even if it means several weeks or months of trying to finally get it.

The 'falls' I have taken in my life in general are nothing compared to the ones I have taken while skateboarding. If you can get back up after a hard fall from skateboarding and keep trying whatever it was that you fell on in the first place, especially when your body and mind are telling you to stop, then you can get back up from anything. Becoming better as an individual and getting through life in general can be just as hard as learning a new trick on a skateboard, if not harder. In either case, you will fall a lot. The same truth that applies in skateboarding also applies to life—if you get back up and keep trying, you will eventually succeed.

If you feel like you are getting knocked down in life right now, keep getting back up. Remember the surge of happiness you get when you finally land a trick after falling and getting back up multiple times to do it. Getting back up in life, no matter how many times you fall or how many obstacles come your way, works the same way. On the other side of rising above any challenges, struggles, or obstacles life may bring is a deep sense of fulfillment and happiness.

Thank you skateboarding, for teaching us how to get back up, no matter how many times we fall.

SUPPORT

One of the things I appreciate the most about the skateboarding culture is the support and camaraderie within. No matter what someone's skill level is, other skateboarders will cheer him or her on and celebrate their victories when they land tricks. Oftentimes, skateboarders will even show support for each other when someone only comes close to landing the trick they're trying. Sometimes the effort alone is worthy of acknowledging.

I witnessed a great example of the support skateboarders give to each other not too long ago. There was a person, about eleven years old, working up the courage to ollie down a double set of three stairs at a local skatepark (Lake Vista in St. Petersburg, Florida—if you're curious). When he was trying to psyche himself up to go for it, each of the six skateboarders at the park started encouraging him. The support helped boost his confidence enough to finally try it. He was not coming very close and started to lose his drive about ten tries in. He went from being confident to looking like he was ready to give up. I could tell he was digging for the motivation to keep going.

He needed an extra push, so I started banging the tail of my board on the ground to hype him up. Within minutes, everyone at the park began hitting their boards on the ground as well. It was awesome! The next thing I knew, the young skateboarder stood up tall and cracked a little smile. He fed off of the support we were giving him. His look of defeat turned into a determined stare. He had made his mind up—he was going to do it! He was fully committed on his next attempt. He cleared the stairs, landed on his board, but fell as he started to roll away. He was so close. Unfortunately, one of his ankles started bothering him badly after that fall, so he called it quits for the night.

Although the young person at the park that night didn't make the ollie down the stairs by riding out of it, he felt the support of everyone there, which is something he will probably never forget. I haven't seen him since then, but I would be surprised if he didn't successfully ollie the double set at the Lake Vista Skatepark the next time he was there. From what I saw, there wasn't a question of whether or not he could do it; it was just a matter of when.

This example is only one of the hundreds I have seen like it over the years. In fact, I watch skateboarders support each other in some way nearly every time I skate. This also plays out when people are competing against each other. Although skateboarders may want to win the contests they enter, it doesn't stop them from getting hyped for someone else and showing support while they are skating.

Think about how many times you have

watched a skate contest like X-Games, Vans Park Series, Street League, or any skate contest for that matter, and you see someone ranked in first place watch another competitor take the lead from them after doing a great run. In most cases, the person that gets bumped out of the lead is more stoked about watching one of their peers have a solid run than they are upset about not winning the contest. The shared respect and support between skateboarders generally supersedes them having any negative feelings toward the person who beat him or her in a contest. Whether skating in a contest or a regular session, skateboarders usually get psyched to see others skating well and want to support each other.

As skateboarders, we all know what it takes to be able to skate in general, to learn a new trick, and how badly some falls we take skating can hurt. We also know how good it feels to get that extra push of support from other skateboarders. When you do land a trick after a long battle with it, or just land something in general, and people start clapping, banging their boards, or cheering, you feel a sense of respect and acknowledgment that sticks with you on many levels. It is never that you do tricks for others' applause, but it does feel great to get it when you do.

There are times I get more joy out of watching someone else land a trick they are stoked on than if I had done the trick myself. When you are standing there to support someone who is struggling to land a trick, you become invested in it as well. It becomes just as hard for you to walk away from the trick as it is for the one actually doing it. I have even experienced this when I wasn't skating and didn't know the people that were.

There was a time I was walking through a town in Iceland with my wife. On our walk, I saw three people skateboarding and one person filming them. My wife and I decided to watch them skate for a few minutes before we continued exploring the town we were in—at least that was the original idea. We ended up watching for much longer.

One of the skateboarders was trying a poll

jam about three feet high at a steep angle with a small gap behind it. Once he got close a few times, I knew it was just a matter of time before he landed it. My wife and I stood there watching with his friends, encouraging him as he worked to do the poll jam and clear the gap behind it. In my mind, I was in the battle with him at that point. I couldn't walk away until he did it. It ended up taking him over an hour to land the trick, but he eventually did. When he finally made it, everyone cheered and seemed equally stoked as he was. It was like we all had done the trick together.

When I walked over to congratulate him and to see the footage his friend captured of him doing the poll jam over the gap, he thanked me for sticking around. I let him know I was happy to do so and didn't want to leave until he did his trick. It was as fulfilling for me to support him during the battle to get the trick as it would have been if I was the one that did it. Either side feels good—being the supported one skating or the one standing there to support someone else skating.

Skateboarding is very much an individual activity but as a collective is one big team looking out for, encouraging, and supporting each other. No matter how down or alone I have felt at different stages of my life, I always feel better whenever I skate with others. Whatever the day's situation, the sense of support and kinship you get from other skateboarders only makes you feel good. Sometimes feeling the support of others and a sense of belonging is all we need to keep going—in skateboarding and in life.

Thank you skateboarding, for giving us so many noteworthy experiences of being supported by, and supporting, other skateboarders.

OVERCOMING FEARS

Skateboarding involves the continuous process of overcoming fears. In any one session, a skateboarder can overcome multiple different fears. Eliminating fear of doing a trick doesn't always happen right away, as we all know. There are times you may roll up to something ten times or more before you get the courage and clarity in your mind to at least try it. Then even when you finally try it, the first few tries are generally not fully committed ones. They are more or less to feel the trick out. Generally speaking, once you get to the point of at least trying it, even though you may not be fully committed yet, the fear you have of the trick slowly starts to diminish. Once the fear goes away, the drive to land the trick takes over.

A good recent example of this for me happened when doing a fakie big spin down four stairs at a local skatepark (St. Pete Skatepark). I had a fear of trying it, so I had to build up my courage first. I skated up to the stairs several times before I did anything. On my first attempt, I more or less popped my board in the half cab motion and jumped down the stairs. Little by little, I started to figure out where to pop my board, the speed I needed, and how to kick my board for the trick to work right. I did this several times before I got past my nervousness of fully committing to landing it. After I overcame the fear in my mind, I started to go for it. The fakie big spin down the stairs took me a little while to do, but I eventually got it.

When you conquer certain fears, they are pretty much gone for good. This is not to say that you won't get nervous or hesitant again when doing the trick you had been afraid to try. However, the initial fear you had of trying it at all won't hold you back again, and over time you get more comfortable with doing the trick. Eventually, you won't even hesitate to do it.

A cool thing about overcoming fears in skateboarding is that everyone's are different. People's apprehensions are based on where they are currently in terms of what tricks they can do, as well as the type of skating they enjoy doing. For example, one skateboarder may be working to overcome the fear of dropping in on a quarter pipe, while another is trying to diminish the fright of doing a blunt to kick flip out on the same one.

Ultimately, mastering your fears is powerful. Whether you still skateboard or not, skateboarding helped, and continues to help, cultivate your ability to overcome any worry your mind creates. Nurturing this type of mental strength and confidence is not only helpful for controlling your angst with certain aspects of your skating. You are also developing character traits that will help you get over any fears that are holding you back from living your life to the fullest extent of your capabilities.

Thank you skateboarding, for cultivating our abilities to overcome any fears that can keep us from excelling in all areas of our lives.

FRIENDSHIPS

Some of my longest-lasting friendships were made through skateboarding. Many have contributed, and in some cases still contribute, more to my life than I can ever give the proper thanks for. Beyond the long-time friends I have from skateboarding, I have also made and continue to make many new ones through skating. I am grateful for all of them.

Some of the friendships you make through skateboarding stay at the skateparks and skate spots. On the other hand, some of them lead to a wide range of different experiences and adventures together. There are even ones who become like family to you. In any case, they are all special.

The excitement and motivation that manifests from a group of friends (a "crew") skating together is such a beautiful thing. I have seen so much amazing skating happen from a crew feeding off of each other's energy during a skate session. When they start feeling the hype from each other, the session keeps elevating more and more. It's epic to both witness and experience the way friends that skate together regularly motivate and push each other. I am always happy to have a solid session with other skateboarders, especially the friends I skate with regularly—they always get me hyped!

Through my many memories of skating with friends, I especially appreciate when our shared bonds and excitement for skateboarding push us all to land a bunch of tricks. There is nothing like when everyone cheers and taps their boards for each other—elevating the vibe of the skate session, together; it's powerful.

I have countless cherished memories of

skating with friends over the years. However, one experience that always stands out for me is a session I had with one of my long-time friends, Jed. We had met in middle school through skateboarding and have been friends since. Years ago, we were skating together at a skatepark when he was visiting our hometown of St. Petersburg, Florida. I hadn't skated with Jed for a while by then, so it was exciting for me to skate with him again. During our session together, we both landed the tricks we were working on for a while, almost at the same time. They weren't the same tricks, but it was still cool to land them, together. It was like we "got each other's backs" without actually calling it out.

Right after we landed our tricks, we looked at each other across the park and nodded. It was kind of like we were saying to each other, "it's on now." The next thing I knew, we both started landing one trick after another. We literally started doing laps around the park landing every trick we tried. He would do a trick, look up at me—I would do a trick, look back at him. We were completely in the zone together taking turns doing tricks, one after another. I can't remember what the tricks were or how many we did. I just know we took turns landing several tricks. I had many great sessions with Jed over the years, but that is one I will never forget.

I bet you have also had such inspiring skateboarding sessions. Take a few minutes to reflect on some of the special moments you've shared with friends who skate with you. If you feel inspired to do so, text or call them to reminisce a bit. The experiences we have with the people we skate with are ones to cherish.

Thank you skateboarding, for being the common thread that gave, and continues to give, us all such cherished memories and great friendships.

OUTLET

My childhood was filled with my witnessing of events that had negative impacts on me. My mom and dad had an unhealthy relationship that involved infidelity, drug addictions, and violence. As I got older, the relationship between my mother and father worsened. My dad eventually left when I was twelve years old, and since then, I only saw him twice and talked to him a few times before I reached my early twenties.

After my dad left, my mom went from one unhealthy dating relationship to another. The 'serious' relationships she had usually only lasted about two years or so. My mom projected a lot of her own pain, confusion, and resentment on my brothers, sisters, and me. She was physically and emotionally abusive to us. My siblings and I were not the best to her either. Over all, the home environment I grew up in was usually hostile.

In addition to the constant fighting and turmoil in the house, my family was poor. There were multiple occasions when our water and electricity were turned off because of the bills not being paid. There was actually a period of time in high school when the water I used to shower came from a gallon jug behind my house. I would wake up around 6:30 a.m. and run to a Seven-Eleven store a couple of blocks from my house to fill the jug with water. After I filled it up, I ran back home to use the water from the jug to take a 'shower' before I went to school. I could go on about different challenges I experienced in my childhood, but I think you get the point—I was dealing with a lot as a young person.

I was so depressed during that time period that I questioned if life was worth living. There were times in high school when my mental health got so bad that I would sit in my bedroom holding the barrel of a pistol in my mouth with my finger trembling on the trigger, squeezing slightly—tempted to pull it. In those moments, I felt like the way to end my pain was to take my own life.

Special note: If you are ever at a point in your life when you feel like suicide is the answer, it is not. Talk to someone about how you feel. Get assistance if you need it. You don't have to do this alone, and there are people that love and care about you. Asking for help is not a weakness—it's a strength. Even if you don't feel like it, keep moving, get outside, and go skateboarding!

Having skateboarding as a healthy outlet during those times, and through many other troubling circumstances I have experienced in life, helped keep me going for sure. Skateboarding gave me the will and desire to keep living, no matter how bad things got. In many ways, skateboarding saved my life, for which I am forever grateful.

I can imagine that some of you may be able to relate to my childhood and the different ways skateboarding helped me to keep pushing through. Whether you can relate to this or not, I am guessing that skateboarding has been, and potentially still is, an outlet for you for different reasons and at different times in your life. Whatever the case may be, it is a helpful outlet to have in your life and is worth making as much time as you can for it.

Still to this day, whenever I am skating, everything gets quiet in my mind, and I feel happy. Things I may be worrying about, overwhelmed by, or processing through, all seem to go away when I am on my skateboard. Skating helps me work through what may be troubling me and also gives me the clarity and inspiration I need in general to live my best life.

Thank you skateboarding, for being a healthy outlet that helps keep us thriving.

PROGRESSION

For the most part, every skateboarder has a desire to progress. Although it may be stronger in some than it is in others, I have yet to meet a skateboarder that is not pushing to progress each time they skate, even if just a little bit. Regardless of what skill level they are at, there is always the drive to do more. As we all know, progression does not come easily. With progression, there are fears to conquer and falls to take. Unfortunately, some of those falls come with injuries.

When you are pushing to progress at

skateboarding, there will always be some type of injury you're dealing with. Some injuries heal in a few days, and some take weeks or months. There are also the ones that never seem to go away. Those are the injuries that get aggravated again every time they start to feel better. I am sure most of you have had an injured ankle at some point that gets tweaked again every time you think it's better, or a wrist that is always hurt because you keep falling on it. Either way, whatever injury happens or however long it takes to heal, most of the time they happen because you are trying to progress. There are the occasions when injuries happen while doing something simple or when you're just messing around. However, those injuries happen more randomly and less frequently than the ones you get from challenging your limits.

Some tricks take a long time to learn, and progression in general is an ongoing process. There have certainly been tricks I've wanted to learn that took me weeks, sometimes months, to get. No matter what it takes or how long it takes, my invested time is always worth it.

Something amazing happens each time you land a new trick and move the needle of progression. Each time it happens, it's like you're unlocking another level of your skating. Every new trick you learn eventually builds into something else. It's a process of progression and desire to do so that never seems to stop.

Whether a skateboarder shouts or screams with excitement, high fives his or her friends, or just rides away quietly and proudly, they immolate a sense of accomplishment that is always inspiring to witness. They conquered fears and overcame struggles, which is always worthy of celebration. In that moment, they are not defined by what they may be dealing with at home or in life in general, if they are sponsored, pro, or not, or what they do to pay the bills. The only thing that matters is the fact that they just landed a new trick for the first time.

In the moments after landing a new trick, especially one you have been working on for a while, you experience what it means to reach new heights and step out of your comfort zone.

You are experiencing progression. You feel stoked, confident, and, on some level—proud.

When you feel what it is to progress and keep proving to yourself time and time again that you can do it, your confidence keeps getting stronger, and you don't stop thirsting for more. It is no surprise to me that skateboarding continues to evolve as much as it does, and that skateboarders are some of the fastest learners and most successful people I know. Many of the skateboarders I have known personally, or know about in general, never quit striving for continued progression and doing what it takes to push their own limits of achievement.

Whether it is on a skateboard, starting a business, pursuing an art (music, writing, design, building, drawing, painting, tattooing, etc.), or excelling in other chosen paths, most people I know or have known that skateboarded for any significant amount of time, or still skateboard, are usually pushing to progress at something. The desire to progress ultimately leads them to many impressive achievements in their lives. Although several variables are involved, I believe the drive for progression that skateboarding brings out in people plays a big role in what they are able to accomplish. I certainly attribute so much of what I have learned and achieved in my life to my 'thirst' for progression that skateboarding has given me.

Thank you skateboarding, for teaching us the value of always pushing to progress and giving us the abilities to do so in all areas of our lives.

FOR THE LOVE

People don't skate for the money, fame, or the ability to acquire material things. They skate for the love of it. Even for the ones who obtain financial success and popularity through a career in skateboarding, that is not why they skate.

Chances are that a large majority, if not all, of the skateboarders who have high-profile careers in skateboarding would still skate if they never got another check or free products to do it. They may not push themselves as hard without the need to do well in contests or to get photos and video footage for their sponsors, but they would still skate. No matter what they may or may not be getting, they love skateboarding.

The relationship we all have with skateboarding is unique to each of us, which is part of what makes it so special. Get ten skateboarders together for a session. They will all be skating together and sharing the hype of the session but will also be having their own individual experience and focusing on their unique craft at the same time.

Each skateboarder will be on different levels and may need skateboarding for different reasons at any one time. For example, as I mentioned before, when I was a youth I needed skateboarding to help me escape from the violence, poverty, and abuse that I was dealing with at home. I needed something I could channel my pain and rage through. As an adult, on the other hand, skating is an important extension to the happy life I now live, not a refuge. Although it helps me work through stuff, keeps me inspired, and benefits my life in so many different ways, there is nothing in my life today that I need to escape from.

This is not to say that either case is limited to certain ages. The point is that at any one time, people will be in different places in their life, and skateboarding will be something that is there for them. Whatever their situation is, or was, people skate because they love it.

Having goals and visions for where someone wants to go with their skateboarding is not wrong at all; in fact, it is common. Ultimately, the love that people have for skateboarding keeps them coming back, time and time again.

Naturally people get frustrated with skateboarding, especially when trying a new trick or having a bad day on their skateboard in general. No matter how mad or frustrated anyone gets while skating, they don't stay that way for long. Skateboarding helps make those that do it become happy and gives them a sense of freedom like nothing else. Even after their worst days of skating, skateboarders are excited for the next time they can do it.

There were times in my life when I had to morn different phases of my skating. I struggled with it for years and would get bummed often. In some ways, it felt like my relationship with skateboarding was falling apart, and I didn't know what to do. For a long time, it was hard for me to let go of the idea of where I once was with skating in my prime.

Although I am working to maintain old tricks and learn as many new tricks as I can, it's different. I tend to respect certain boundaries now that I didn't have when I was younger. In other words, I am no longer doing tricks down big sets of stairs like I once loved to do. It took me awhile to be okay with that. In fact, I think one of the reasons I stayed away from skateboarding the times when I did is because I was not letting go of the past. I would get more bummed and hung up on certain things that I had once done on a skateboard versus being able to really enjoy my time skating in the present.

Now, although I still challenge my limits on a skateboard, I do my best to embrace the gratification that skating brings me, no matter what tricks I am doing or not doing. In order for me to finally find my peace with the different stages of my skateboarding, I had to check in with the most important part of skating—the love of doing it. The reality is that we will all go through different phases of our relationship with skateboarding. It's important that we always remember why any of us skate in the first place, which is the love we have for it.

If you are an older skateboarder (late twenties and above) and feeling at all discouraged to skate or get back into it, don't worry about where you once were. Assess where you are now, what tricks you have and don't have, the tricks you want to be able to do, and challenge yourself to progress from there. Let yourself fall in love with being on a skateboard again. On the other hand, if you are younger (mid-twenties and under) and still actively skating, keep at it, take it all in, and enjoy the ride. Either way, whatever your skill level or age is—be sure to have fun, push whatever you feel your limits are, and keep skating as much as you can. Above all, don't ever take what skateboarding has given to you, and will continue to give you, for granted.

No matter what level any one is skating at, our love for skateboarding is only understood in its entirety by others who skate. Sure, people can appreciate it and even grasp it to an extent, but it's hard to understand completely unless you experience it for yourself. In some ways, I think the reason skateboarding sessions feel so sacred is because we are all sharing in something we love, at the same time, together.

Thank you skateboarding, for being a love that brings us together for so much goodness in our lives.

CLOSING STATEMENT

Whether you are still skating or not, skateboarding will always be a part of who you are, which is something to be proud of and grateful for. Let's give thanks to skateboarding for the many positive ways it has, and does, impact our lives.

OTHER BOOKS BY RICKY ROBERTS III

- *You* (2004)

- *What Really Matters?* (2006)

- *Where Did the Gift Go?* (2009)

- *Awakening the New You: A Path to Transformation* (2013)

- *Just for Youth (2015)*

- *Healing the Wounded Child Within: Heal Your Wounds Change Your Life* (2018)

- Far Fom Easy: What It Takes to Make Your Dreams a Reality (2019)

Made in the USA
Las Vegas, NV
03 February 2021

17081239R10046